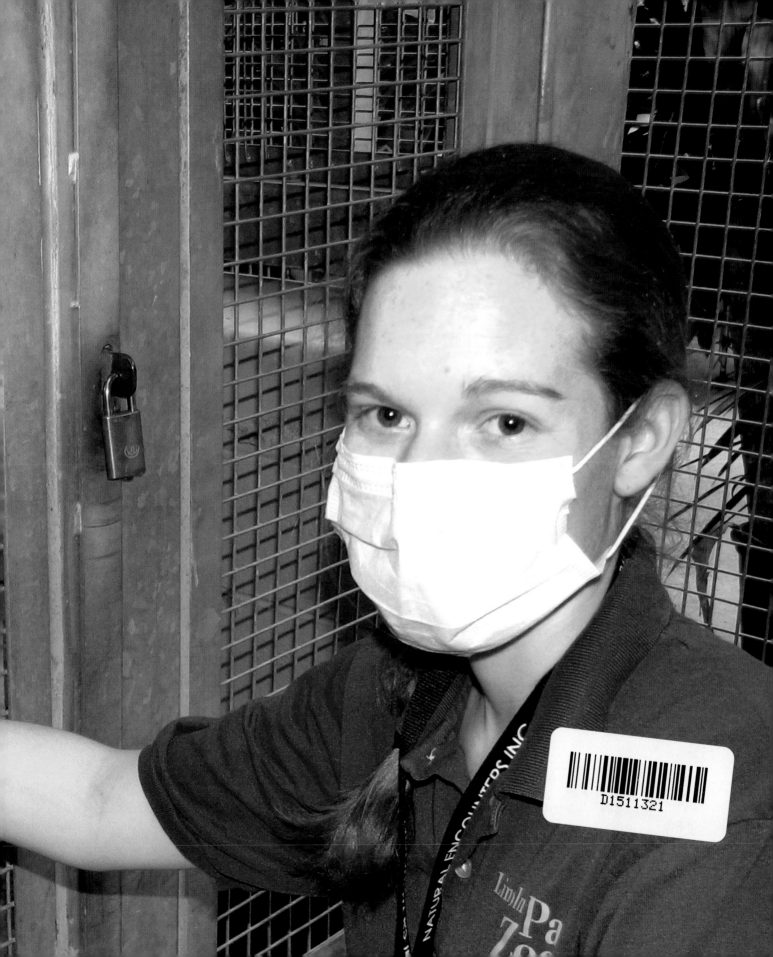

Open your mouth so I can check your teeth, Kwan, Dominic signals. "Good," says Dominic. He rewards the silverback gorilla with a frozen blueberry.

Time to play, Christopher. The orangutan reaches out one hairy arm to gently tap the touchscreen. He completes the memory game. "Good boy, Christopher. Here's a treat!"

Animals that live in zoos don't perform tricks. Much like children in school, they study important lessons. In training "classes," the animals learn behaviors that keep them happy and healthy.

The swamp monkey, gorilla, and orangutan live in the zoo. They are primates. Primates are a type of mammal. Like other mammals, they are warm-blooded, have hair and backbones, and make milk for their young. But primates have some traits that other mammals don't.

Primates use their hands and feet to grasp objects. They have fingers and toes. Most primates have eyes on the front of their faces. They can see color. Babies take a long time to grow up. They need adult primates to take care of them. Most live in groups or troops. They play and eat together. And primates are *smart*.

Bornean orangutans

siamang

Allen's swamp monkey

Sumatran orangutan

There are more than 500 species of primates. Some, like pygmy marmosets, are the size of your hand. Male gorillas grow bigger than most people. And humans are primates too.

white-cheeked gibbon

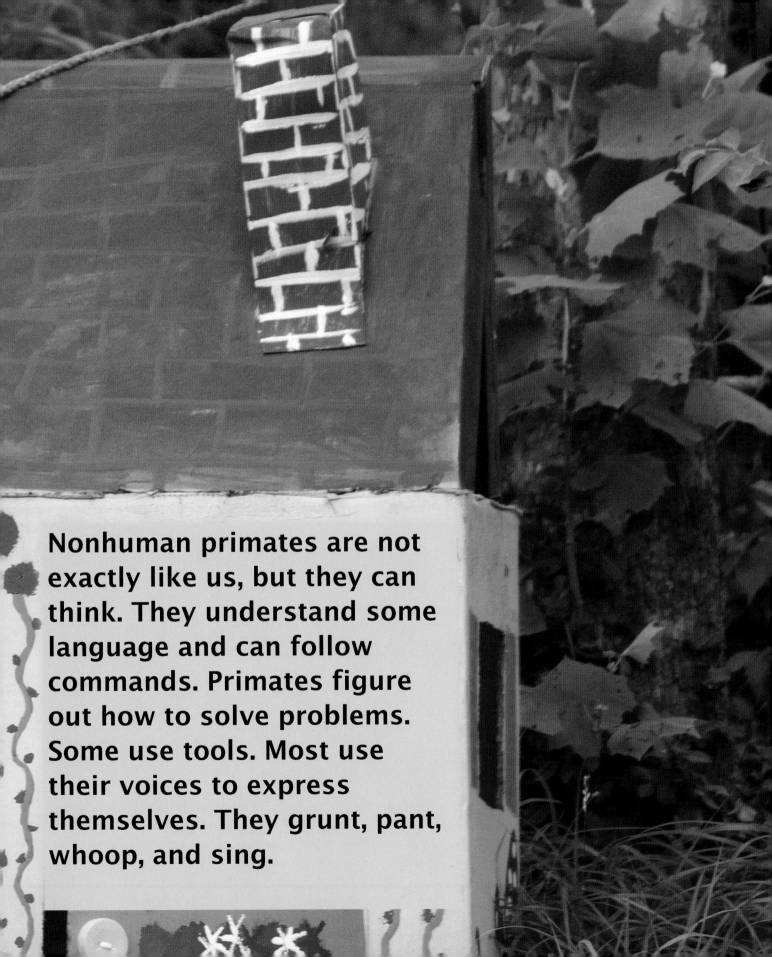

Nonhuman primates are not exactly like us, but they can think. They understand some language and can follow commands. Primates figure out how to solve problems. Some use tools. Most use their voices to express themselves. They grunt, pant, whoop, and sing.

western lowland gorillas

In the wild, primates learn from members of their group. They discover ideas by exploring, observing, and playing.

Sumatran orangutans

François' langur

In zoos, primates still learn from each other. Keepers also teach them.

western lowland gorilla

chimpanzees

squirrel monkeys

Allen's swamp monkey

Why are primates in zoos?

Zoos help preserve endangered species, like orangutans. Zoos also rescue and provide homes for primates born in labs or sold as pets.

Like other wild animals, primates do not make good pets. They are very strong and difficult to handle. They may bite. In zoos, keepers don't get into the enclosures with chimps, orangutans, and gorillas.

western lowland gorilla

red ruffed lemur

Scientists and keepers work hard to understand as much about the animals as they can. In the wild, primates are always busy and learning. They think about gathering food, where they will sleep, and with whom they should play.

golden lion tamarin

Keepers use this knowledge to create natural habitats that help the animals feel at home.

white-cheeked gibbon

Since most primates are very social, they live together in the zoo. Just like in the wild, they groom and help each other.

siamangs

François' langurs take care of each other's babies.
This is called *aunting behavior*.

Keepers also encourage wild behaviors.

An Allen's swamp monkey looks for tasty leaves, buds, and bugs.

Chimpanzees use tools—sticks— to "fish" for termites.

A gibbon sings.

A lemur hangs upside down to eat.

Enrichment is an important part of the primates' day. Keepers provide food, fun activities, and even touchscreens. These help vary the animals' routines. Sometimes the primates play like kids at recess. Enrichment keeps them happy and healthy and encourages them to think and problem-solve.

A gorilla pokes bananas out of a plastic puzzle board.

A squirrel monkey pops bubbles.

Lemurs paint.

A gorilla plays a game on a touchscreen.

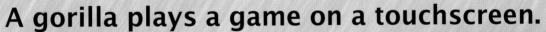

Keepers are like teachers. Their daily lessons for the animals are fun and keep everyone safe. But training sessions are voluntary. That means the primates don't have to take part if they don't want to.

red ruffed lemur

With target "class," keepers train the animals to come, go, hold still, touch, and stay. The primates learn to come to the target and touch it with their hands or noses. The animals are intelligent. They know they will be rewarded—with applesauce, raisins, or dried fruit—for cooperating.

howler monkey

Primates also learn to stay in one place. The animals hold still so that the keepers can touch them if necessary and make sure they are healthy. This is called stationing.

In some zoos, keepers train primates for medical check-ups. Orangutans and chimpanzees learn to show their chests so that a vet can listen to their hearts with special equipment.

Gorillas place their arms into special sleeves for blood tests. Because the animals work so hard, they get a big reward called a "jackpot," such as extra juice or a large chunk of banana.

white-cheeked gibbon

Now that you know how smart nonhuman primates are, do you think one could survive your school day?

For Creative Minds

Primate or Not?

Primates come in all shapes and sizes. A pygmy marmoset weighs only 3.5 ounces (less than a smartphone). A gorilla can weigh over 400 pounds (as much as a piano). But even though there are many types of primates, they all share certain traits. Using the list of traits below, identify which animals on this page are primates. Answers are below.

All primates have:
- fingers and toes.
- the ability to sit or stand upright. Most primates can walk on two feet (bipedal) for small distances. Only humans walk on two feet for most of their life.
- eyes on the front of their face.
- a reduced sense of smell and smaller noses than other mammals.
- a heightened sense of sight. Most primates can see color.
- large brains for their body size.
- babies that take a long time to mature.
- longer lifespans than other mammals.

Almost all primates have opposable thumbs. "Opposable" means that the thumb bends in a different direction. This helps the primate grab objects.

dog

Allen's swamp monkey

human

turtle

elk

siamang

horse

gorilla

Primates: Allen's swamp monkey, human, siamang, gorilla

Endangered Species

Dinosaurs. Woolly mammoths. Eastern cougars. Baiji river dolphins. We know of animals that once lived on this earth but have disappeared forever. They are extinct. Some animals today are not extinct, but may become extinct soon if we don't help them. These animals are called endangered species. An animal's conservation status (chart on the right) can tell you if that species is in danger of extinction.

Almost half of all primate species are endangered or critically endangered. This happens because of habitat loss, poaching, and hunting. Without help, these animals could also become extinct.

Many zoos and sanctuaries support conservation efforts to help save these animals. These include protecting natural habitats, caring for injured animals and releasing them back into the wild, teaching people about endangered animals, and working to prevent poaching.

You can support conservation efforts too! Learn about endangered species all around the world. Pick up litter so animals don't eat it or get trapped in it. Participate in "citizen science" programs. You can find these through your local zoos, wildlife sanctuaries, parks, nature centers, or a government agency responsible for protecting the wildlife in your area (Department of Natural Resources, Wildlife Resources, Fish and Game, etc.). These will help you learn about endangered animals in your area and how to help them.

LC—Least Concern:
A species that is not currently at risk of becoming endangered.

NT—Near Threatened:
A species that may become endangered in the near future.

VU—Vulnerable:
A species that will soon become endangered unless people do something to change the situation.

EN—Endangered:
A species in trouble. It may become extinct if people don't help.

CR—Critically Endangered:
A species in dire trouble. It is likely to become extinct without immediate help.

EW—Extinct in the Wild:
A species that only lives in captivity. The species still exists only because people take care of it.

EX—Extinct:
A species we'll never see again. Extinction is forever.

chimpanzee
status: EN

françois' langur
status: EN

white-cheeked gibbon
status: CR

ring-tailed lemur
status: EN

siamang
status: EN

blue-eyed lemur
status: CR

Sumatran orangutan
status: CR

western lowland gorilla
status: CR

Talk Like a Chimp

In the primate family, chimpanzees are one of humans' closest animal cousins. Humans and chimps have a lot in common. Like humans, chimps live in groups, make tools, work together, and take care of each other. They use sound, gestures, and facial expressions to talk to each other and show how they feel.

Chimps use different sounds and calls to talk to each other. They whimper, scream, bark, and grunt. Different sounds have different meanings, like words do for people. Chimps say "hello" with a sound called a pant-hoot. Just like your voice sounds different from other people's, every chimp's pant-hoot is unique. That way, the chimps know who is making the sound, even if they can't see each other.

> **Say "hello" like a chimp:** Make an "o" shape with your mouth. Breathe out and make short, hooting "oo" sounds.
>
> What are some ways you use sound to communicate?

Chimps use their bodies to communicate. They stamp their feet, hug, swing their arms, jump, tickle, and scratch. Chimps tell each other to come closer by beckoning with their arm or by grabbing and pulling. They stick out a foot to tell young chimps, "climb on me." If a chimp wants to say "back off" to another chimp, they punch the ground or wave their arms.

> **Say "stop that!" like a chimp:** stomp both feet or gently tap whomever you are telling to stop.
>
> What are some ways you use your body to communicate?

Chimps make many different expressions with their faces, just like people do. If they are frustrated or want something, they scrunch in their eyebrows and make an "o" shape with their lips. If they are afraid or excited, they bare their teeth.

> **Say "I feel playful" like a chimp:** relax your face and smile with your mouth open, like you are about to laugh.
>
> What are some ways you use your face to communicate?

Enrichment

Animals in the wild are always busy learning. Zookeepers know what primates do in their natural environments and give them opportunities to learn in their enclosures. They create a schedule so they can continually change activities and keep the animals interested.

Food is an important source of enrichment. The animals love treats but the keepers have to make sure that the animals don't get too much sugar. Snacks include: nuts, unsweetened oatmeal, rice, seeds, and dried fruit. The food may be hidden in a box or toy so that the animals work to find it. In the summer, keepers and volunteers freeze juice to make healthy popsicles for the primates.

gorilla

hamadryas baboon

golden lion tamarin

ring-tailed lemur

Allen's swamp monkey

Like kids have jungle gyms at recess, animals have enrichment items in their habitats. These can be platforms, perches, swinging ropes, hanging feeders or places to hide and to dig. The primates jump, play, swing, and climb on the objects in their enclosure.

Primates love to play, just like human children do! Toys give the primates new objects to learn about and explore. The animals play with Kong toys and examine jigsaw puzzles. They snuggle stuffed animals and carry large boomer balls.

white-cheeked gibbon

white-cheeked gibbon

white-cheeked gibbons

siamang

hamadryas baboon

Thanks to the following experts for sharing their knowledge in interviews with the author: Dr. Steve Ross and Curator of Primates Maureen Leahy, Lincoln Park Zoo; Keeper Sabrina Barnes, Nashville Zoo; Keeper Margaret Rousser, Oakland Zoo; and Keeper Kristina Krickbaum of Zoo Atlanta.

Thanks to the following people and organizations for sharing their expertise and photographs with us:
· Adam Thompson and Marietta Danforth from Zoo Atlanta (zooatlanta.org)
· Amiee Stubbs (www.amieestubbs.com) from Nashville Zoo (nashvillezoo.org)
· Nancy Filippi, Daniel Flynn, Colleen Renshaw, and Dannielle Stith from Oakland Zoo (oaklandzoo.org)
· Richard Zimmerman and Colleen Reed from Orangutan Outreach (redapes.org) and Center for Great Apes (centerforgreatapes.org)
· Photo of Gober & the Twins complements of Jessica McKelson from the Sumatran Orangutan Conservation Programme (Sumatranorangutan.org)
· The P.R. Department at Lincoln Park Zoo (lpzoo.org)

Cover Image: Siamang Hanging from Tree, 208535365, used under license from Shutterstock.com

Library of Congress Cataloging-in-Publication Data

Curtis, Jennifer Keats.
  Primate school / by Jennifer Keats Curtis ; with Lincoln Park Zoo, Nashville Zoo, Oakland Zoo, Orangutan Outreach, and Zoo Atlanta.
     pages cm
  Audience: Ages 4-8.
  ISBN 978-1-62855-555-4 (English hardcover) -- ISBN 978-1-62855-564-6 (English pbk.) -- ISBN 978-1-62855-582-0 (English downloadable ebook) -- ISBN 978-1-62855-600-1 (English interactive dual-language ebook) -- ISBN 978-1-62855-573-8 (Spanish pbk.) -- ISBN 978-1-62855-591-2 (Spanish downloadable ebook) -- ISBN 978-1-62855-609-4 (Spanish interactive dual-language ebook) 1. Primates--Behavior--Juvenile literature. 2. Primates--Training--Juvenile literature. 3. Zoo animals--Training--Juvenile literature. I. Title.
  QL737.P9C889 2015
  599.8--dc23
                                    2014044579

Translated into Spanish: *Escuela para primates*
Lexile® Level: 670L
key phrases for educators: animal classification, primates, tools and technology, zoos

Bibliography
Antle, Bhagavan, Thea Feldman, and Barry Bland. Suryia Swims!: The True Story of How an Orangutan Learned to Swim. New York: Henry Holt, 2012. Print.
The Ape Who Went to College. PBS. Television.
Braun, Eric, and Sandra Donovan. Tamarins. Austin, TX: Raintree Steck-Vaughn, 2002. Print.
"Chicago Zoo Creates Gorilla-blood Database." Chicago Zoo Creates Gorilla-blood Database. AlJazeera America, 17 June 2014. Web.
Donovan, Sandra. Howler Monkeys. Chicago, IL: Raintree, 2003. Print.
Esposito, Stefano. "Chimps Use Special Tools to Raid Hives for Honey." Chimps Use Special Tools to Raid Hives for Honey [Chicago] 22 Mar. 2009. Chicago Sun-Times. 22 Mar. 2009. Web.
"Great Ape Heart Project." Great Ape Heart Project. Web.
Halloran, Andrew R. The Song of the Ape: Understanding the Languages of Chimpanzees. New York: St. Martin's, 2012. Print.
Hatkoff, Juliana, and Peter Greste. Looking for Miza: The True Story of the Mountain Gorilla Family Who Rescued One of Their Own. New York: Scholastic, 2008. Print.
Hobaiter, Catherine et al. "The Meanings of Chimpanzee Gestures." Current Biology , Volume 24 , Issue 14 , 1596-1600.
Janega, James. "Zoo Chimps Reveal New Ideas about Innovation." Zoo Chimps Reveal New Ideas about Innovation 11 Nov. 2013. Print.
Meinelt, Audra, Ryan Gulker, Ann Ward, and Barbara Henry. "Colobus Monkey Care Manual." COLOBUS MONKEY. Web.
Nagda, Ann Whitehead, and Cindy Bickel. Chimp Math: Learning about Time from a Baby Chimpanzee. New York: H. Holt, 2002. Print.
"News." Orangutan Outreach: Reach Out and Save the Orangutans. Orangutan Outreach. Web.
Orme, David. Orangutan. Chicago, IL: Heinemann Library, 2005. Print.
"Planet of the Apes." The Economist. The Economist Newspaper, 15 June 2013. Web.
Sodaro, Carol. "Chapter 15 Positive Reinforcement Training." Orangutan Species Survival Plan Husbandry Manual. Chicago: Chicago Zoological Park, 1997. Print.
Spilsbury, Richard, and Louise Spilsbury. A Troop of Chimpanzees. Chicago, IL: Heinemann Library, 2003. Print.
Stewart, Melissa. Baboons. Minneapolis: Lerner, 2007. Print.
Waal, F. B. M. De. The Age of Empathy: Nature's Lessons for a Kinder Society. New York: Harmony, 2009. Print.
Waal, F. B. M. De. Our Inner Ape: A Leading Primatologist Explains Why We Are Who We Are. New York: Riverhead, 2005. Print.

Manufactured in China, January, 2015
This product conforms to CPSIA 2008
First Printing

Arbordale Publishing
Mt. Pleasant, SC 29464
www.ArbordalePublishing.com